AF481146

How did we get here?
Musings of a 45-year couple
By Dennise Demming & Richard Demming

Published by Dennise Demming and Richard Demming
Diego Martin, Trinidad & Tobago

Editor: Adeline Gregoire
Cover photography and design: Patrick Rasoanaivo
Layout design: Patrick Rasoanaivo

ISBN 978-976-8291-66-0

Foreword

The legacy of friendship

By Maxine Barnett

"Good friends are like stars, you don't always see them but you know they are there."
Friendship that stands the test of time, distance and generation is to be cherished.
As a witness at your wedding, I was there to see the beginning of your forty-six years years of marriage and special friendship.....a test of time!
Our friendship of over 46 years has stood the test of distance.
Our children, the next generation: Keita & Quincy and Jeanine, Kisha & Kara... now adults, continue their friendship, a bond which began when they were toddlers... a test of generations.
We are now privileged and blessed to see our children's children, the next, next generation and have a front seat as we share this legacy of friendship.

Introduction

One idea can save someone's relationship.

This book is about stories that made us remain together and values by which we lived. Some of them go against conventional thought and traditional behaviour. After 40 years, we kind of got tired of having celebration parties and so this book is a way to share the stories of our lifetime, our lifetime together and our relationship.

Richard's parents, Hannah and Oliver Demming celebrated 51 years as a successful Caribbean couple, navigating an English environment in the 1950's and challenging the traditional norms of their generation. Oliver died in 1999 and Hannah in 2021. We believe that the transference of their values has played a major role in the lives of their four children who are also experiencing long marriages.

As Richard approached "three scores and ten", he reflected on his life's journey and some of the values that guided him. Some of his musings included:

- Growing old is better than the alternative.
- We should exercise moderation in all things, including moderation.
- As an Engineer, the easiest part of problem-solving for humanity, is the engineering ie. the design component.

After two years of collaboration, our thoughts have become "Musings of a 45-year couple" and so here we are. Much of the content for these stories was unintentionally provided by our two sons, Keita and Quincy Demming.

The stories in the book generally reflect the chronology of our lives. We have come to a place of accepting that the relationship is always more important than any argument, and knowing which battles to fight. Fighting is usually seen as aggressive, but fighting can also be done in a warm and friendly way. It does not always mean resorting to fisticuffs.

We have many young people in our lives who are not biologically our children but whom we regard as our children and we wanted them to have a reference point.

As lifelong learners, it is our hope that current and future generations will be inspired to work towards deep, meaningful relationships.

Photo credit: *Mark Lyndersay, 2008*

*Painting by Artist Naveen Lalla (Trinidad & Tobago), 2019
Demming Art Collection*

Acknowledgements

We would like to thank Hannah Demming for seeing a future for us that we did not necessarily see. For our wedding day, Gillena Cox designed and created our wedding outfits which perfectly reflected our support of the burgeoning 70's Afro-Trinidadian culture in Trinidad & Tobago. Carol Slusher, Dennise's flatmate at that time, sang *The Wedding Song (1976)* originally performed by Captain and Tennille. The words of the song resonated deeply for us on that day, and still do 45 years later.

Over time, there are a few people who have impacted our lives in different ways. We'd like to say special thanks to Maxine Barnett, the late Ina Nicholson, the late Lauriston Lewis, Alex and Heather Heron, Dr. Vanessa Stewart and the late David Neale, Lynette Shepherd, Stephen Seepaul, Hilton Barnett, the late Dave Elcock, Ivor Ferreira, Joanna Collymore and The North Stand Panorama Crew.

We thank the following persons who have brought joy to our lives:

Bri Celestin, who adds feminine energy to our lives and is a loyal friend;

Greg and Liz Stone, for their joy, fun-loving spirit and for being good cooks;

Wendy Hoyte, an anchor, neighbour and loyal friend;

The late Alvin Alexander, Richard's mentor;

Camille Parsons, for her generosity and for being a place of comfort;

Annette Knott, a friend for life;

Christlyn Moore, who is brutally honest and always there for a reality check;

Christine Norton, Dennise's friend from school;

Gillian Seecharan, a fun loving, beautiful voice;

The late Alfred Alfred Patrick, a goal setter

and Kenycia Doyle, a future thinker.

Dedicated to the memory of

the late Hannah and Oliver Demming
the late Rita and Claude Romany

the future of

our sons Keita and Quincy,
our grandchildren,
Taniesha Marsden and
Oliver Demming
And future generations.

About Dennise

Dennise came from a single-parent home in East Dry River, Port of Spain and credits all her success to the unconditional love she received from her mother, especially during her early childhood years.

Dennise left Holy Name Convent with four O'Levels and over the years has earned three degrees: a BSc, an MBA and an MSc.

She is passionate about positively changing Trinidad and Tobago and finds inspiration in interacting with creative, restless persons. As a communications practitioner, change agent, event organiser and teacher she is committed to making a difference wherever she lands. Dennise believes that effective communication is the vehicle to release our creative energies for our mutual benefit.

Her current passion is to engage couples and help them maintain healthy, positive relationships.

About Richard

Richard was born in San Fernando and left Trinidad for England at the age of four. He was the second West Indian to attend an all-white grammar school in Chorley, Lancashire. His brother Robert was the first. Richard had a fairly successful sports career and represented his University in football and athletics. In 1973, he was ranked among the top ten 400-metre runners in Britain.

Richard is a builder, he likes making things and is good with his hands.

After graduating as an engineer and working for two years in London he returned home to Trinidad. Richard later switched to the insurance business where he worked for over 30 years. He now leads a Human Resource Company. Throughout his life, Richard has been involved in volunteerism and currently serves on two non-profit boards.

How did we get here?

Musings of a 45-year couple

Dennise Demming & Richard Demming

How did we get here?

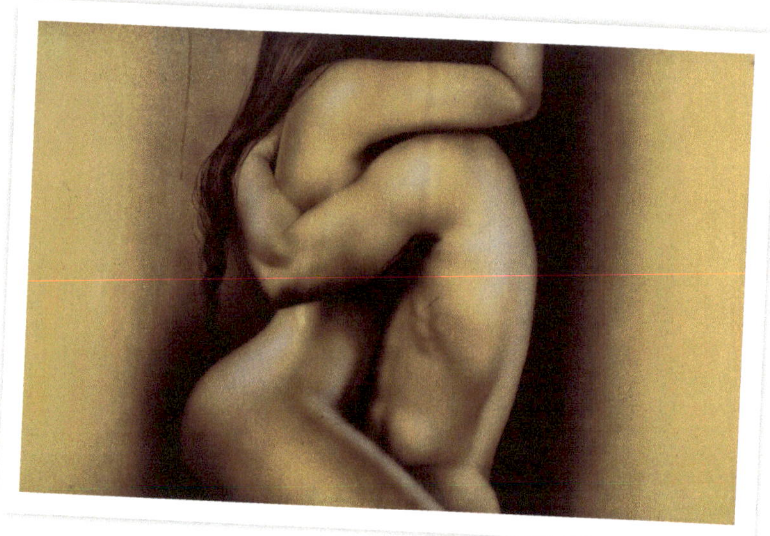

Painting bought at a market in Rio de Janeiro (Brazil), 2002
Demming Art Collection

Wait three months for sex

I met Richard at a time when we were both searching
for a meaningful relationship. I had seen "Lady Sings
the Blues" for five nights consecutively, with five
different men and knew that was not what I wanted.

We agreed to get to know each other before becoming
intimate and made a pact that there would be no sex
for three months while we got to know each other.

What we learnt

We learned about each other and discovered qualities which
we liked. Looking back, we both agree that this gave us a strong
platform for the future.

Dennise as a race car driver, St. James, Trinidad & Tobago, 1977

Independent Dennise

Soon after we began dating, Dennise moved out of her mother's home and began sharing an apartment with one of Richard's friends, Carol. As time went by Dennise would spend more of her time at Richard's apartment. We agreed however that until we were married we would each retain our separate apartments.

Life lesson

It was important to us that when Dennise stayed at Richard's apartment it was by choice and not out of necessity.

How did we get here?

On our Wedding Day, 21st January 1977
Arima Presbyterian Church, Trinidad & Tobago

Size of the wedding

We had been dating for about one year when we visited my mother for Christmas Breakfast and he told her that I had agreed for us to get married. I ignored the statement but when we met his parents for lunch later that day, he told his mother the same story. Up to today I don't remember him asking me to get married!

I wanted a small, quiet wedding at the Red House which is where town hall marriages occur in Trinidad and Tobago. Richard's mother Hannah intervened because in her opinion "if it is not done in a church it is not done properly." Within five weeks Hannah arranged a Friday afternoon wedding at the Arima Presbyterian Church. All we had to do was show up.

My girlfriend Gillena Cox made our outfits and our neighbours Hilton and Maxine Barnett were the best man and chief bridesmaid. Dennise's flatmate Carol sang the "Wedding Song". There were maybe 12 people in the church and 24 people at the reception which Hannah arranged at her home.

The Benefit

We began our life together debt free and were able to travel over the next five years without much consideration for the costs.

How did we get here?

Series of Despers T-Shirts owned by Richard and Dennise

Wedding Party after 2 years

We showed up for the Panorama "North Stand lime" and were severely heckled because many of our friends were disappointed at not being invited to the wedding. So, for our 2nd Anniversary, we held a big party for those whom we did not invite to the wedding. It was necessary to acknowledge that our friends wanted to be part of our journey. After two years of being together we recognized that we really had something to celebrate.

The Benefit

We learnt two things: firstly, the importance of celebrating the marriage and not necessarily the wedding as an event. Secondly, our friends have always supported us throughout our journey as a couple.

How did we get here?

Managing our Irish twins while looking professional, 1986

Get the cakes in the right order

We noticed that many couples who had a child before being married often did not remain together. We coined the phrase "get our cakes in the right order" meaning that we should have the wedding cake before the christening cake.

The Lesson

It is extremely important to be psychologically ready to have children and to plan for their arrival.

God, grant me
the serenity
to accept the
things I cannot
change, courage
to change the
things I can,

Serenity Prayer

and wisdom
to know the
difference.

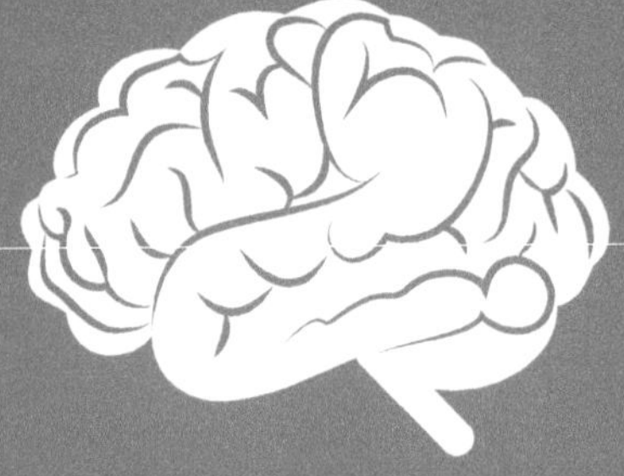

Contentious Tenancy

We rented a house for a year during which time there
were issues with the landlord. On the last day of
the tenancy when he came to inspect, an altercation
ensued and he hit Dennise with a cushion. The next
thing Richard recalled was Dennise shouting his name,
trying to get him off the landlord and to stop choking
him! It took seven shouts for Richard to hear Dennise.

Life Lesson

No matter what the circumstances, you need to control your
emotions. Our life mantra since then has been "respond,
don't react."

How did we get here?

Building a foundation
for children

During the early years of our marriage, we moved house several times. We observed and often said to each other that "man is the only animal which has its young before building its nest". We did not want to repeat that. Therefore, we decided to work towards buying a house before starting a family. This took us five years to achieve.

The Benefit

These five years allowed us to strengthen our foundation - in a literal and figurative sense - before introducing another human being into our life.

"The relationship is more important than the argument."

When to stay and when to go

Our relationship suffered a seismic shock early in the marriage. This caused anger, pain and mistrust but also provided an opportunity for deep reflection and a resetting of the boundaries. It was followed by what seemed like a week-long conference in which there were nightly discussions of the "whys" and "hows". While the adults were working through the issue, the inner child in each of them longed for connection. Eventually a "treaty" was "signed" and the work began on rebuilding trust, establishing new protocols and working on reconnecting as partners in the relationship.

Life Lesson

To accept that relationships are tested when there is an unsatisfied need. Couples then need to decide if the relationship is worth saving.

How did we get here?

When under stress, communicate more. A moment for ourselves while Dennise was coordinating the passage through Trinidad and Tobago of the World Cup Jules Rimet Trophy in 2014.

The 3 Cs

We've always had a good sense of each other but
there came a time of frequent misunderstanding
and conversations would end with both of us feeling
unheard.

It prompted one of us to comment that while we both
made a living through communication, we were getting
it wrong between ourselves. From that moment, we
made a greater effort to communicate,
by seeking more feedback from each other.

Life Lesson

The 3 Cs of our successful marriage have been
Communication, Communication and... Communication.

How did we get here?

Mortgage Burning Party

Finish the room then celebrate

In keeping with our philosophy of celebrating
achievements, while constructing our new home,
we had a small celebration every time we completed
a part of the house and invited friends over.

Remember

It is important to celebrate the small wins.

How did we get here?

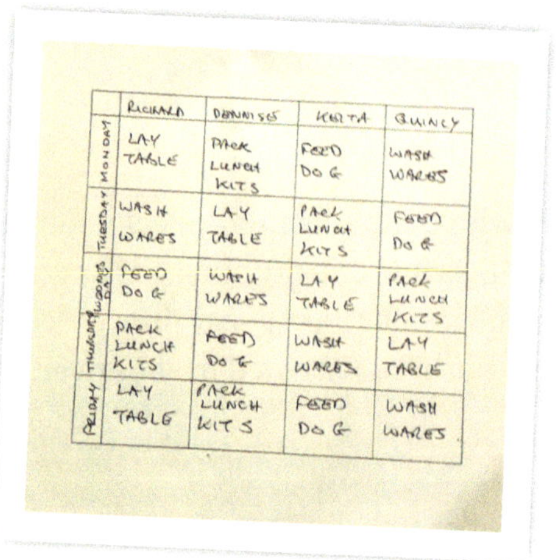

	RICHARD	DENNISE	KEITA	QUINCY
MONDAY	LAY TABLE	PACK LUNCH KITS	FEED DOG	WASH WARES
TUESDAY	WASH WARES	LAY TABLE	PACK LUNCH KITS	FEED DOG
WEDNESDAY	FEED DOG	WASH WARES	LAY TABLE	PACK LUNCH KITS
THURSDAY	PACK LUNCH KITS	FEED DOG	WASH WARES	LAY TABLE
FRIDAY	LAY TABLE	PACK LUNCH KITS	FEED DOG	WASH WARES

A typical roster of chores in our house.

A roster for chores

As two aspiring professionals in our twenties and
thirties, managing the household was becoming
onerous so we employed a helper to take care of the
home. As soon as the children could walk, we created
a roster of chores which was rotated on a weekly
basis. This helped us to add structure to our lives and
accomplish our dreams.

The Lesson

Structure in your life provides space and time for seizing
opportunities.

How did we get here?

We are eternally grateful to The Harvard Sports Club, which had a major impact on our children's growth and development for about 10 years.
Photo credit: Patrick Rasoanaivo, 2023

Sunday sports

From ages 4 and 5, our sons spent their Sunday mornings until noon at the Harvard Sports Club and played whatever sports that were being conducted. They were both outstanding sportspersons and excelled on the field of play. One even went on to wear the national colours for the Under 19 Rugby Team of Trinidad & Tobago.

Reflection

Sunday morning sports taught our sons discipline and exposed them to persons from different backgrounds. They also met sportsmen who were giving back by being positive role models, passing on their knowledge.

How did we get here?

A chance meeting with an Artist by the name of Sellier led to this beautiful family portrait, inspired by a Garth Murrell photograph.

Sunday lunch

A strategy used to manage the household was to have a family meeting after lunch on a Sunday, and one of the rules of those meetings was that you could change any rule or policy once you presented a reasonable case which we, as parents, could buy into. Our sons often collaborated on the things they wanted to achieve. Unbeknownst to us at the time, they also had pre-meetings to establish their objectives.

Reflection

We continue to be proud that our sons learned the benefit of teamwork and are both great collaborators in their lives.

How did we get here?

Richard's tool box

Building a Buggy

Richard used to build go-carts when he was a boy. One Sunday, he decided to show our sons how to build a buggy, a dear memory of his childhood. He basically ended up building it himself but when it was finished, the boys in the neighbourhood had great fun with it.

Life Lesson

Many times what you see as a good idea may not resonate with your children, but they may come on board... after the hard work is done.

How did we get here?

Presentation College, Chaguanas, Trinidad

When teachers complained ...

"WHY?" was a question that was encouraged in our home and both of our sons took that question to school. It became a problem in secondary school since they were often seen as challenging authority when they asked "Why?" We were frequently called to the Principal's office because of some apparent challenge to the administration.

Benefit

Our sons learned to stand their ground and knew that if they were presenting a logical challenge, we would support them.

Don't knock it

until you try it.

How did we get here?

Becoming The Man of the Series in Guadeloupe

One of our sons had his sixth form examinations which clashed with the Regional Under 18 Rugby Tournament in Guadeloupe and he wanted to play for the National Rugby team. He knew he could not do both but he was confident that rugby was more important for him at that point. In the face of his determination, we had no choice but to support his decision. He was also such a dedicated player that when one of the selected players was unable to get his passport issued in time, our son became the obvious choice to join the team. Overjoyed, he went to Guadeloupe and was awarded Man of the Series.

Reflection

Some opportunities in life have a short window and we need to have the courage to seize them when they are presented. Most importantly, we have to believe in ourselves when conventional wisdom says otherwise.

How did we get here?

Travelling the world...(Top to bottom)
Our first trip to Caracas, Venezuela in 1978
Visiting friends in Stratford on Avon, UK in 1979
Oh how we loved the Leaning Tower of Pisa! Italy in 2000

Experiences last longer than things

We lived a very simple life and our children did not enjoy the latest in fashion, toys or games. We preferred to save and spend our money on vacations in different places from next-door Tobago to Europe and as many other places as we could afford.

Reflection

Our aim was to expose our sons to different cultures and to help them understand the importance of prioritising things in life. We are not sure that these lessons stuck, but at least we certainly tried.

Mt St. Benedict, Trinidad, 2013
Photo credit: Patrick Rasoanaivo

Richard and St. Benedict

After fifteen years as an Engineer, Richard was contemplating a career change and needed some time to reflect. A friend recommended that he spend a few days at Mt. St. Benedict, a mountainside Monastery in Trinidad which had a retreat house. During this time Richard attended a 5:00 am church service, exercised every morning on the playing field before having a simple breakfast and also assisted with some small construction projects. One of the Monks, Brother Pascall Jordan was assigned as his mentor. He found it a very enlightening experience which allowed him to put many things into perspective.

Life Lesson

Disconnecting completely from the life to which you are accustomed can bring tremendous clarity and open up new possibilities.

Anniversary postcards from our friends over the years...

Celebration Time every 5 years!

As a young couple, we could not afford a big anniversary celebration every year, so we preferred to hold a wedding anniversary celebration every five years.

Reflection

Over the years, each celebration has provided an opportunity for us to reflect, reset and Determine our direction for the future. In addition, celebrating significant achievements can give you encouragement to strive for more.

How did we get here?

Our boys Quincy and Keita (L to R) at their grandparent's home in Champs Fleurs, Trinidad & Tobago, 1987

Participation vs Observation

Our philosophy with gifts was to buy things which promoted a healthy lifestyle. This meant that our children did not get the latest amusement toys but rather they received bicycles, surfboards and many other games which encouraged physical activity.

Life Lesson

Our sons realised that they could not get everything that their friends got, but their gifts would give them many hours of pleasure.

How did we get here?

Painting of Indica smiling (Quincy's pet) by Artist Akilah O'Brien, 2020

Pets. Even if you don't like them.

Neither of us was particularly fond of animals, but we felt we should allow our sons to have one if they wished. During their childhood to teenage years, we have had 3 family dogs.

Reflection

Our sons learned how to take care of other living beings which had minds and attitudes of their own, and one of them has a dog today.

How did we get here?

Bread as QBA

Dennise failed one of her courses - Quantitative Business Analysis (QBA) while reading for her MBA. She was totally devastated and needed to remind herself that she could succeed at many things, so decided to go back to something she knew how to do well: bake bread. For a long time in our household, home-made bread was called "QBA".

Life Lesson

The simple act of baking bread (or doing something that you are proficient at) can be a reminder that you can achieve anything you wish if you put your mind to it.

How did we get here?

Group photo with Dennise and the TTRRC
Always running! One of Dennise's many races

Staying healthy

Dennise remembers being at the top of her career and enjoying the success and recognition that came with it, but one year, the results of her annual medical showed all the numbers going in the wrong direction. We knew that she needed to make significant lifestyle changes. We changed our diets to include more fruit and vegetables, she picked up running with the Trinidad and Tobago Road Runners Club (TTRRC) which she continues up to today and has already completed 9 marathons.

Life Lesson

A healthy lifestyle trumps any success you may have in business.

How did we get here?

From First Class to Economy...

From 5 stars to 1 star

When our boys were still in their teens, we booked a family vacation in St Maarten using our Time Share at a 5-star resort. When the time came to leave, we were advised that no flight could land because of the threat of a hurricane. We would be staying in St Maarten for two more days. We found a small hotel which was miniscule in comparison to the resort, with zero facilities - no gym, no tennis court, not even located on the beach - and stayed there until we were able to leave the island.

Years later one of our sons recalled the incident and concluded that we were broke, from what he saw as a "step down" in the quality of the accommodation. He did not say anything at the time but became more reflective on what he asked of us.

Reflection

The experiences you give your children will affect them in ways that you may not see until years later.

Getting ready for camp!

One year, we decided to send the boys off to their first overnight summer camp for ten days. We went through a ten-day programme with them. Each day ended with "lights out" and then "sleep". After repeating this for 10 nights in a row, Dennise was packing their suitcases for them to leave the following day for the first day of camp. Thinking out loud, she said: "the only things that we still need to pack are the pyjamas."

One of the boys then asked: "Are we going to sleep there?"

Reflection

Sometimes you think you have communicated when you really have not. Despite our ten days of preparation, our children did not understand that they were getting ready for an overnight camp.

Maracas beach, Trinidad & Tobago, 2020
Photo credit: Patrick Rasoanaivo

Maracas Beach

Taking care of two boys - Irish Twins - demanded a lot of energy and was sometimes frustrating. At times, Dennise just needed to chill and discovered that sitting on Maracas Beach provided an excellent opportunity for our sons to discover the joys of the ocean and for her to simply relax. Our boys both went to swimming classes from 3 months old, so we were comfortable by the sea although Dennise couldn't swim.

Reflection

It is necessary as a parent to find activities which involve you and your children without putting too much pressure on anyone.

Uncle David
Uncle Cecil

Aunty Ina
Aunty Maxine

Aunty Vanessa

...

Acquired Aunties and Uncles

None of these persons are biologically related to us but our children called them and several others "Aunty and Uncle".

Aunty Vanessa scolded one of our sons for hanging out of the window of a maxi-taxi while they were leaving a Carnival fete and for calling her out as "Aunty Vanessa". She gave him permission to drop the "Aunty" when they were in a fete.

Reflection

"Aunty" or "Uncle" was a mark of respect which we encouraged our children to show to our close friends. It is a valuable cultural tradition which seems to be disappearing from our society.

How did we get here?

Spot the fisherman!

Children's careers

When it came to our children's choices of a career, our position was that "you could do anything you want, but it must begin with certification", so that you can be the best at whatever you attempt.

Today one of our sons works as a Leadership Consultant. Our other son whom teachers always described as "brighter" is a certified Mechanic, Diver and Fisherman. For us, both are now successful in their respective fields.

Reflection

It is necessary to let your children find their own path.
We accepted that our children were able to excel at anything that inspired them.

How did we get here?

Keita Demming
University of Toronto, 2016

In theory and in practice

The house we now live in is on a hill and a dozen or so metres above the road. At the start of construction the supplier left 300 bricks on the roadside. Richard offered one of our sons 50cent per brick to move them up to where the house would be. Our son gladly accepted the challenge, and he and a friend eagerly began the task. They moved the first 150 bricks in 30 minutes. The second 150 took 90 minutes.

Later that day our son explained he'd finally understood that a math problem could be approached theoretically or practically. That experience made him opt for the theoretical approach and he resumed his Education and went to school for the next 14 years. Today he has a PhD.

Life Lesson

There can be some unexpected consequences when you give your children a task to do. In this case it was a very positive outcome.

How did we get here?

Our respective family homes in Lancashire, England and Quarry Street, Trinidad.

Create your own culture

Rita and Claude were Dennise's parents and their marital relationship was marked by domestic and alcohol abuse. Richard came from a very stable home environment created by his parents, Hannah and Oliver. Between the unconditional love Dennise experienced from her mother and the many valuable lessons Richard learned from his parents, they were able to piece together a stable relationship which has endured the passage of time.

Life Lesson

While family background or the "family of origin" shapes people, it is important to create your own values and culture for your marriage to thrive.

How did we get here?

Pre–wedding family gathering on an African winter morning in Botswana.

Life is short.
Buy the flight ticket.

One of Dennise's childhood friends moved her family to Botswana. One year in advance Richard and Dennise received an invitation to the wedding of one of her daughters. Their immediate response was that they could not afford such a trip. A few months before the wedding, another friend who was stunningly beautiful and successful, died of cancer. This prompted them to reflect deeply on the uncertainty of life. They changed their minds and went to the wedding in Botswana. Their friend Joanna appreciated their presence and their visit left them culturally enlightened.

Life Lesson

Life is short and there are some opportunities you should not miss.

How did we get here?

The boys: Keita and Quincy, in preparation mode for one of our family meetings

A united front to respond to children.

Children enter your life as little people with their own thoughts, views and aspirations. It is almost instinctive for our little angels to try to drive a wedge between their parents and caregivers. Our children were particularly good at trying to play one against the other in order to achieve their individual goals. We had to learn very quickly to consult each other before providing a final decision. On their end, they also learned quickly to team up to achieve their objectives.

Reflection

Collaboration is important to achieve your objectives, at every stage in life.

*School days: Keita and Quincy in front of our first home in
Chaguanas, Trinidad, 1993*

Trust your role as a parent

One day a friend called to offer congratulations on the excellent work our sixteen year old son was doing at the YMCA after seeing a Newspaper story about him volunteering at a homework centre. We were stunned because he was supposed to be at Briar House studying after school and we were unaware of his work at the YMCA. When confronted, his response to us was: " You don't trust how I was brought up?"

Life Lesson

After putting in the work of nurturing your children, have the courage to back off and allow them to thrive.

How did we get here?

Perspectives from Kilimanjaro

David Neale (deceased) was one of our closest friends and had been planning a trip to climb Mount Kilimanjaro in Tanzania and we decided to join him. Unfortunately we chose to abort the climb on the second day because Richard developed a medical problem. While David made it to the summit, we used the time to go on a safari through Ngorongoro Park. On our way back home to Trinidad & Tobago, we also spent three days in Dubai. Moving from extreme poverty to dinner in Burg Al Arab during that trip, moved us to think about inequity, and what we could do to reduce it.

Reflection

We observed the vast discrepancy in the conditions under which people lived in different parts of the world. This helped put our own country's situation into perspective.

Welcome

Making Home the preferred place for their friends

We had an open door policy for our children's friends who came to lime, have fun, relax and spend time. As a result they always felt comfortable being at our home. When all the friends were together we did not have to worry where our children were and whether they were safe. Their friends' parents were also comfortable knowing that their children were being well taken care of.

Reflection

Not only was it a convenient solution for us as parents, doing this gave us peace of mind, knowing where our children were. We also wanted our children's friends to know that our home was a safe and welcoming space.

How did we get here?

*Bubbling a pot in the kitchen of our first home in Edinburgh Gardens,
Chaguanas, Trinidad*

Don't open Gema's pot!

With the birth of our first son and the addition of our second son 13 months later, life changed dramatically. We chose to hire a housekeeper to assist with managing our house and children so there could be a better balance of energy between our careers and home life.

We were blessed by the presence of Gema who worked with us for many years. She fitted in place as the de facto "manager of the house", and felt so empowered that even our children's friends had to ask permission to open Gema's pot.

Life Lesson

Everyone sets their own boundaries, it is important to make them known so that others will avoid crossing them.

Understanding each other's strengths

While doing an MBA, Dennise had a problem with a question in Quantitative Business Analysis (QBA) and asked Richard if he could help. Richard looked at the question and showed Dennise how to approach the answer. This infuriated Dennise because Richard had not even read the associated chapter of the book. He simply used his knowledge and proficiency in mathematics to solve the problem.

Life Lesson

It is important to understand that people's abilities interlock with their life experiences to give them their unique blend of strengths. This difference can be seen as a way to make a stronger team, rather than letting it cause a rift.

Rum

& Ginger

How did we get here?

Dark sky, Aripo, Trinidad & Tobago, 2022
Photo credit: Patrick Rasoanaivo

Rain is a state of mind

When our sons wanted to cancel or postpone some activity because of the rain, Dennise would say to them: "Rain is a state of mind, so do what you have to do." Gene Kelly's hit "Singing in the rain" happens to be a favourite in our household. One day, on the way to Maracas Beach, it was raining heavily and Dennise wanted to return home. The boys insisted that she carry on and reminded her that "...rain was a state of mind!"

Reflection

Be careful what you instil in your children, it may come back to you when you least expect it!

How did we get here?

Sailing away…

Giving each other space to be who they want to be

As time went on Richard became less interested in Carnival. Dennise however, was totally inspired by the revelry and joy, so Richard agreed to do the drop-off and pick-up from Carnival Fetes. Cell phones were not as common back in the early 2000's so they had to agree on the time and place for each pick up. One Carnival Saturday morning after the Soca Monarch Finals, Dennise was picked up on the foreshore (fortunately she had prepared her travel outfit) so they could head to the airport to catch a flight to spend the Carnival week sailing.

Life Lesson

Relationships thrive on trust, openness and understanding each other's needs.

Over the years, we have always shared our projects with our children, whom we see as great team players.

Involving your children

The entire family often worked on Dennise's projects especially when she started her own business. Our sons were strongly encouraged and rewarded for their contribution. One year, she was contracted to create and implement a "Summer Camp", and used it as an opportunity to expose our sons to coordination and facilitation. Today they are both involved in training as part of their careers.

Reflection

Children learn what they live. It is important to be intentional in what you expose your children to.

How did we get here?

Keita Demming
10 December 2018 ·

Mom asked dad to buy ginger on his way home. He wasn't sure what she meant so he got two very important kinds of ginger. This is how you stay married.

— with **Dennise Demming** and **Richard Demming**.

Social media post from Keita, 2018

... *And the Two shall become One.*

Dennise has created a lot of discussion amongst friends with her statement: "I like my husband more than I love him".

This statement goes back to our wedding ceremony, when Rev. Clyde Persad, now deceased, said "...and two shall become one". What he did not say is that the "oneness" might take decades to manifest.

We finally realised that Rev. Persad's statement on our wedding day took several years to take shape, and today the two of us - have finally become one.

Reflection

In "Becoming One" there is less anxiety between us and we approach issues in a solution focussed way. Our mantra is that the relationship is more important than the argument.

How did we get here?

Be healthy, Be happy!

Over the course of 45 years together, we experienced the passing of some very dear friends and saw others experience a decline in their quality of life. The most important thing for us is to remain as healthy as possible. In addition to exercise, a healthy diet, rest and relaxation we seek continuous mental stimulation.

Life Lesson

Intellectual activity contributes to our healthy lifestyle.

How did we get here?

Conference and Mediterranean Cruise in Barcelona, 2000

Cruising the Mediterranean

While Richard was in the insurance business, the company held biennial conventions overseas and the agents could qualify for themselves or qualify to attend with their spouses.

One year the trip included a cruise and Richard was behind the target set for him. At breakfast, one morning Dennise announced that "Daddy has only qualified for himself to go on the cruise". Thereafter the morning question became: "Daddy, is Mummy on the boat yet?"

That year, we both went on the cruise and enjoyed every moment of it.

Life Lesson

Motivation comes in various shapes and forms. No father wants to look inadequate in front of his sons.

How did we get here?

The Retirement Map

We both opted out of the corporate structure early in our careers. As a result we were not subject to the usual schedule of a fixed retirement age. This decision gave us the impetus to map out what we thought our retirement should look like and when, if ever, it would happen. Today at 67 and 72 years of age, we both continue to be active in the world of work while enjoying our financial freedom.

Life Lesson

It is possible to chart your own model of success, find what works and have the courage to follow your heart.

Let there be spaces

Khalil Gibran

in your
togetherness.

All Stars Carnival
East Dry River Port of Spain,
Photo credit: Maria Nunes, 2013

How did we get here?

Reviews of "How did we get here?" Musings of a 45-year couple

by Dennise Demming and Richard Demming

How did we get here?

By Gillena Cox

Oftentimes, when you meet a contented couple of long-standing years of marriage, you want to ask: How did you do it? Well, the musings of this Demming couple give us the much-desired information.

In a candid, conversational tone we are privy to the reality of this couple's success.

Presented in a series of short chapters, which I prefer to call panels, each panel ends with a Life Lesson.

As I read through, images jump out at me: values, celebration, and legacy in a constantly flavoured blend of 'we'. Here is a journey embarked upon by two adventurers who value friendships and inspiration.

After reading their musings, I rejoice in the knowledge that success is something to be shared, not harbored. I "luv" their passion for keenness in planning and their willingness to inspire us with the wisdom achieved along the way. "No matter what the circumstances, you need to control your emotions". I simply adore this Demming and Demming mantra, from the chapter 'Contentious Tenancy' and also, from the chapter 'Children's Careers' … "It is necessary to let your children find their own path."

'How did we get here?' seems to be echoing the reader's curiosity, rather than the couples' question. Bravo and well done! Dennise and Richard Demming. This lovely little dossier on meeting, marrying and marinating is a legacy for every couple intending on a success story.

Photos and other illustrations add to the aesthetic reading of this book.

By Robert Demming

A very personal recollection of a lifetime of experiences within the personal and family environment and with very important reflections which touch us all. Interestingly, rather than being purely an account of the past, the 'musings' delve into the 'why' and the 'purpose'.

Not all is plain sailing but the direction is onward and upward and the actions thoughtful. The message is unmistakable, the family matters, sticking together matters, and life is often 90% perspiration but take the opportunity when it arises. It is also clear from the 'musings' that family is all around and that realisation only strengthens the journey for all concerned.

One is left with a sense of what can be achieved despite the ups and downs of life and that with a positive approach, there is much in life to be thankful for.

By Heather and Alex Heron

It is a brave couple that decides to scrutinize its 45 years of marriage. Some would say, foolhardy! Do you open cans of worms? Do you peel the onion only so far? Do you admit to irresolvable failures? After a lifetime of root-planting do we even recognise these? After all, just because we, who are a longtime married, "made it" does not mean that we "lived it"; that we did not fundamentally sacrifice something of our core selves in the process of two becoming one.

Dennise and Richard manage, with some success, to navigate this minefield of reflection. They allow us to dip into their backgrounds, their successes, and into some of their dark times. In trying to answer, "How did we get here?" they rightly try to offer answers in the form of advice to the next generation embarking upon coupledom and family life.

The granite foundation of their marriage is hewn from a rich seam of lived experiences in England, Trinidad and the wider world. Their story is underpinned by striving. It is about education; about a well-intentioned rational approach; about rising above poverty and setbacks. Above all: of Carpe Diem.

Their book has the feel of a tantalising starter. The musings are rooted in psychology, in aspiration, in experiences, in life's compromises - with Trinidad and England as the exciting and formative backdrop. It is potentially a huge story. Perhaps Richard and Dennise's brave dissection of lessons learned from a long marriage will embolden them to analyse further in future publications?

By Mark Lyndersay

This little book tells a big story. Two young people from Trinidad and Tobago find each other, choose a life together and forge success for themselves and their two sons. This is not as commonplace as it should be, particularly in Afro-Trinidadian families. I know this, because I am writing these words in my office, once the bedroom where my father told my mother that he was leaving her. I was seven.

Making mistakes in romance can be a crushing reality. I've clocked a divorce and two failed long-term relationships in my own past.

Dennise and Richard have been in my life for all those experiences and I like to think that watching them steadfastly and collaboratively forge ahead with their lives taught me to be a better person – perhaps one that my wife might occasionally like to have around.

Even knowing them for four and a half decades, this book packs a punch. The remembrances they share are a gentle but inspiring reminder that love is easy, but a happy, rewarding life takes work.

By Kimiko Scott

While witnessing Dennise and Richard navigating the last 10 years together, questions like this book's title have indeed come to me repeatedly. How do they do it? How did they develop their ease of communicating? What is their secret?

With models of good relationships being hard to come by, "How did we get here - Musings of a 45-year couple" feels like a welcoming door being opened for readers to gain insight into this fascinating and inspiring couple's journey. Lessons learned as individuals, a couple, and a family are shared in an astute, relatable manner.

Weaved within their reflections, a beautiful success key emerges: marital longevity may require the willingness to learn each other deeply and the wisdom not to lose yourself in the process.

www.ingramcontent.com/pod-product-compliance
Lightning Source LLC
Chambersburg PA
CBHW040944110726
48006CB00007B/1248